THOUGHTS ON A PAGE

RICKEEM RICHARDO JONES

ACKNOWLEDGEMENTS

Where do I begin? I wouldn't even know where to start or how to even go about giving thanks to the people who have helped shape me into the person I am today. I adore the people who have guided me. Without certain people, I'm sure my life would not have turned out the way it has.

For the people close to me, and I mean the people I'm in contact with on a daily basis...the people who can see how much effort and focus I put into what I am doing - I f**cking love you with all my heart and I don't say that lightly. You have inspired me beyond your own awareness, through you being you I've understood what it means to be a true friend. Although I am a leader in my own right, I feel no way when it comes to following your guidance.

Mother. This woman is my everything. If I could show you the lengths this woman has gone to in order to support and provide for me, it would bring tears to your eyes. She is the definition of inspiration, a source of unconditional love. I admitted to myself a long time ago, that no way would I ever be able to repay all she has provided me with. I know I talk about impossible but if there is one thing I think is impossible, it's this.

It exceeds money and materials. It travels far beyond anything physical. I chose instead to represent her in the best way I can, I want to show her what an amazing job she has done. I want her to see the rewards of her sacrifices. I want her to know that her efforts have contributed to me being an inspiration to others. She pursued her own dreams whilst raising me and finding the drive to still turn up every day and give it her everything.

I'm in awe and I forever will be. Mum, you know I don't play when it comes to my goals and the things I set my mind to. I tell you all the time...you've raised a champion.

Love Rickeem x

Love to Zain, my advisor, the genius who introduced me into the world of creativity. His ideas, energy and support have made this book more than what I could of done alone. You will forever have my support and I look forward to watching you weave Seven Quarters into the fabric of fashion history.

Achievable Ways Of Living x Zainwoos

"To live beyond the pale, to work for the pleasure of working, to grow old gracefully while retaining one's faculties, one's enthusiasms, one's self respect, one has to establish other values than those endorsed by the mob. It takes an artist to make this breach in the wall. An artist is primarily one who has faith in himself. He does not respond to the normal stimuli: he is neither a drudge nor a parasite. He lives to express himself and in so doing enriches the world."

Henry Miller

CONTENTS

Welcome. It has been a long time coming and I'm proud to say the time has finally come. I wholeheartedly thank you for deciding to purchase this book. I send you all my deepest gratitude, and please, I encourage you to reach out and personally give me your feedback on how this book has impacted you and changed your perspective of what's possible.

For around six years now, I have taken the time to thoroughly explore my thoughts in great depth and use them as a form of therapy and expression. I began to realise almost instantly that through writing, I was able to articulate my emotions in a way I verbally couldn't. I found an outlet that allowed me to connect with myself and analyse my current state of mind. This gave me a clearer understanding of my thought process and where I was at emotionally. Since writing, I've been able to share my deepest thoughts in a non-judgemental environment as the page does not judge, criticise or doubt. It only listens and reflects. The freedom I felt to be able to express, knowing my words are automatically understood, set me free from the fears which have previously held me back.

In 2015, I made a decision to commit to finding as many ways as I can to bring out the best of me and leave my stamp on the earth. My goal is to leave behind enough of me to live on through generations, whether that is through the content which you are reading or through the belief in which I am able to instil into people. Will this happen? Who knows! All I can do is go for it wholeheartedly and the results and outcome will speak for itself. Writing this book has not only kick-started my journey towards becoming an author, it has also allowed me to express and share with the world my thoughts and view on life, which have allowed me to live with courage, belief and most importantly love.

This is what fuels my inspiration; to continue towards bringing out the best of me. There were times whilst writing this book, when I had thoughts of cancelling the project. My motivation would fade, life would get in the way, momentum and my focus would slip causing me to lose interest in the process. It has been a love and hate relationship between me and the experience, thankfully with love always coming out on top.

Although it has been a difficult process, I've enjoyed it so much, enough to start working on a second book project. There isn't too much to report on that just yet. Just know it's in the making. During the process of writing this book, I've learnt creative work comes with an element of obsession. The artist or creator may have a desire for minimalism, perfection and order of perspective. In my case, it's simplicity - "less is more." I aspire for my work to contain less but produce more. With that in mind I've created the format and layout you will see within this book. It's a style that suits my philosphy and should be easier for you, as the reader, to digest and implement.

You see..I immerse myself into what I put my mind to. I become it. It's part of my obsessive nature. I get emotionally connected to what I'm creating. I have this belief that energy invested creates value. Although it can't be seen, always go the extra mile because it can always be felt.

On that note, I'm going to wrap up this introduction to allow you to travel this extra mile and enter the thoughts of my mind to get an insight into how I process, decode and piece together life. I want you to extract from this book what you find is beneficial and combine it into your own way of thinking for the purpose of improving the quality of your life. Without futher ado, lets get this ball rolling.

Before I let you dive into the energy which awaits you, I have a short exercise for you to take part in. You can call it a mental warm-up, a little something to get your brain waves firing and your inspiration flowing. My aim is to have you progress through this book in an empowered state of mind and right *here* is where that journey begins. Let's get to it.

Repeat each affirmation twice for two rounds.

I AM beautiful, I AM magnificent. Even if I don't believe it, I am going to keep repeating this to myself until I have no choice but to believe it because I AM.

I CAN and I WILL.

I AM strong, I AM determined, I AM resilient and I AM everything it takes and more.

I commit to giving me the best of me.

I AM in the process of becoming the best version of myself.

Repeat these affirmations to yourself until you are feeling fired up and ready to go. Say it with your chest and speak with conviction. I want you to say it like you mean it because you do. Get a taste of belief, you are light, you are energy, you are everything. Let's go!

ACHIEVABLE WAYS OF LIVING

After that warm-up, how are you feeling? What are your thoughts on you? Tell the page. There are no rules, you are free to express however you please, I just encourage you to write something meaningful and reflective. I have ensured that you start this book in an empowered state. I'm now asking you to lead by example and set the pace by writing something about yourself worthy of putting a smile on your face, not just today, but whenever you decide to come and read this book again, there will be a beautiful message about you, from you and to you.

MY POSITIVE THOUGHTS ABOUT ME

_____

_____

_____

_____

_____

_____

_____

_____

_____

_____

SIGNATURE: DATE:

CHAPTER 1:

PERSONALLY SPEAKING...

"This is the world in which I belong. The world of expression, creativity, inspiration and mastery. The world which is slowly being left behind. This place is my home. We pursue audacious goals and fight worthy causes. This is the world of truth and fulfillment. I want to remain here, as life here seems to be a beautiful manifestation of what the visionaires of this forgotten world have created."

ACHIEVABLE WAYS OF LIVING

Although this path may be a lonely road to travel,
in spirit i am not alone as you are with me.

"Let me get all these truths and worries out of my system. Let me put this pain into writing so I can physically see it. Now it is no longer trapped in my mind, it has been set free into a place of understanding."

ACHIEVABLE WAYS OF LIVING

Whenever you start feeling overwhelmed, pour your energy into an outlet. Be it in writing, singing, colouring, dancing or working out. Do your best to ensure it doesn't just remain trapped within you. The longer it stays within you, the more deep rooted and heavier it becomes. Search for an outlet that is suited to your character and get expressing yourself.

"I don't want to force these words, only express when it feels natural. It's clear to see this is a unique part of my character. When the words start flowing, it's as if they could last forever. It's fantastic and I cannot wait for the day I have books of my own for book worms like myself to absorb. That, right there, will be my success".

ACHIEVABLE WAYS OF LIVING

Once I'm in a state of flow nothing exists. It's like a place beyond this realm. Words, inspirations, ideas pass through me. When I'm in the zone I'm introverted and don't want to break the train of thought. There is no desire to eat, drink or even move once I get into my peak state of writing.

I have no desire to switch off. I love living with intensity, it's my place of creation. All that I create is for the purpose of inspiring — I pray my journey as an author impacts lives across the globe and my books reach the hands of those who appreciate, need and value the integrity of my work.

"Years of emotions are wrapped up in these pages. Hundreds of mixed thoughts collected and used as a reflective strategy and healing mechanism."

ACHIEVABLE WAYS OF LIVING

If it wasn't for discovering writing, who knows what my outlet would have been. This has been a life saver. I wasn't even expecting it to manifest in the way it has done. I didn't once think I would be writing a book. Until recent years, this was not even a thought.

I find it fascinating how things prevail, especially when there is no agenda or intention other than expressing and just going with what is. Opportunities and ideas materialise. Naturally it takes a shape of its own and if you see room to take it to another level, it only makes sense to do so.

"My thoughts need to be explored and my nature needs to be expressed. A life not lived to its full potential, is one I struggle to even comprehend or enjoy. Not because I don't value life, but to have the best experience from life, I've got to have the best drawn out of me."

ACHIEVABLE WAYS OF LIVING

Love to all those who are of the same feeling. Keep at it, even if you are in an environment where you are not being stretched to the best of your ability. Take the initiative to take it upon yourself and bring out the best of you.

We haven't got time to waste. Life is running out. We are doers and doers do, regardless of the circumstances. Whenever you can, do your best to ensure those you are surrounded by are playing their part and trying to also bring out the best within themselves.

"The beautiful thing is that I don't have it all figured out and you know what? I probably never will. Life is too complicated to solve all the problems and issues we face. It's best to find which strategy is best suited for you to persevere and keep learning in this journey called life."

ACHIEVABLE WAYS OF LIVING

People are easily overwhelmed when it comes to the complexity of life. They stress themselves by over-complicating issues that are better left flowing and figuring out as you go along. Life is too short to try and figure it all out. Let life be life, nobody has it all figured out and not many know what they are doing as good as they may make it seem.

Trial and error is a concept worth keeping close to you. There is no shame in admitting that life can be a hot mess at times for each and every one of us. Nobody has it easy in life, so please don't for a moment think that life is purposely targeting you. It's a sticky mess for us all. Do your best to make the most out of a bad situation. Have faith in yourself.

"I know what it is like to live with doubt. I understand what it is to live with fear. I used to believe that I wasn't good enough to become someone in this world. One thing I did realise is that for all that negative self-talk to stop, I, myself had to make the effort to change."

ACHIEVABLE WAYS OF LIVING

I want this experinence to be as real and raw as I can keep it. I've had my fair share of doubtful moments along with many other fearful times. Nights I have tossed and turned questioning almost every aspect of my life. Lost in the whirlwind of a negative spiral.

It wasn't until I drew the line, the thoughts were way too much; no way could I deal with it for a moment longer. I pulled myself together and figured out what needs to be done and went ahead and attacked it directly, and here you are, reading the results of my efforts, the fruits of my labor. If you are looking for proof as to how things improve and how you can become someone significant in this world, it's in your hands this very moment.

"I have been facing a couple of mental battles recently – internal confrontations. The usual battle of Me vs. Me. You would be glad to know, I won."

ACHIEVABLE WAYS OF LIVING

And this is always going to be the outcome. I will always win when it comes to the battles within. Affirm this to yourself. Make it known that you are the conquerer of you.

This is where the fuel is generated. The many battles conquered with self. There is a balance between being firm and also, being compassionate with yourself. Once that balance has been found, you will see how to remain in control of your emotions and not be beaten by yourself.

"I have developed a serious urge to push myself in areas I am extremely uncomfortable with. The confidence gained from such acts are highly valuable."

ACHIEVABLE WAYS OF LIVING

Why do things you are not comfortable with? What sense does that make? Well, to see what you are able to accomplish, you have to test yourself in areas where your weaknesses are exposed. What more are we learning from taking part in disciplines that we know we will excel at?

Challenge yourself in an area where you have no experience and minimal knowledge. Human beings find fulfilment and happiness when we witness ourselves grow through the result of our own efforts.

"If I tell you about a goal that seems audacious, don't assume that I, as the person that I am today, is going to achieve that goal. Think ahead, who I am now is a snippet of who I'm becoming."

ACHIEVABLE WAYS OF LIVING

Operate with the long-term in mind. Be aware that it is going to take a greater YOU to achieve a greater goal. If there is ever a time I explain an audacious aspiration, work with me and help me develop into the person I need to become to achieve that goal.

Sorry, but I don't want to hear how it can't be achieved! That is not the energy or attitude I want around me. Let's bring to the table the energy to inspire the possibility.

"I cannot wait to love. It penetrates my whole being. To dive into the emotion with a fearless attitude excites me. To be emerged with another beautiful soul...my gosh, it sets a smile upon my face. The opportunity to be able to give the best of me in exchange for receiving the best of her...how can such a wonderful insight not be smiled upon? Man, the day I am set free upon the woman of my dreams will be a moment in human history."

ACHIEVABLE WAYS OF LIVING

Human connection is the essence of life. When two souls collide, the earth shakes. What contributes to a successful connection? Beyond the basic fundamentals of loyalty and respect, there is a secret sauce. A special ingredient located in the centre of your heart. You find that, and the moment you align with another soul who has found their sauce...boy oh boy, you are about to witness something electrifying.

"This love of mine is dangerous. Once you get a taste of this raw uncut emotion, I promise you'll never experience a love like this again. You may experience more, even less but it will be nothing close to this."

ACHIEVABLE WAYS OF LIVING

Looking back, I used to be so reserved and kept my emotions firmly tucked away. As soon as I had a taste of what love is like compared to what I perceived it to be, boy did it change me!

It introduced me to a side of myself that I wanted to see more of. I now know I love deeply and I'm confident enough to express my emotions and I encourage more men to embrace their feelings.

Love is not something you are to rush or force. Let it develop organically. Two souls operating on the same frequency, rowing in the same boat, going in the same direction. Only then, can love take shape and produce greatness.

"Sometimes it's hard to articulate and express this gratitude I have within me. I can only write and hope that the energy I feel is attached to the page. So for whoever reads this, your vibration is raised as you are reading something that has stemmed from truth."

ACHIEVABLE WAYS OF LIVING

I will always give my thanks and share my energy. Live to be raw in your truth and connected to something that keeps you grounded and aligned with your morals. There are times I receive an overwhelming sensation of gratitude — so much so that I don't know what to do but I give thanks by putting it into writing.

Looking at it now, there is proabably a strong reason as to why I express the way that I do. It's beyond my control. Even if I tried, I think it would be extremely difficult to keep all this within me. I believe I've unlocked the gates to inspiration. If I can continue to use and share my energy in positive ways you will not for a second catch me complaining. Aim to live with an attitude of gratitude.

"I am an example to myself that dreams do come true. So whenever there is a day that I am struggling to believe, I come back to this message to remind myself: life works in beautiful ways."

ACHIEVABLE WAYS OF LIVING

It's incredible when you become your own inspiration, when you can reflect upon your journey to date and feel a sense of gratitude and accomplishment. Only you can see the internal battles you have had to conquer behind closed doors when you are faced with yourself. Only you can see the many mountains you have climbed and the obstacles you have overcome. It's a beautiful sight, right?

Rarely do we give ourselves enough credit. We don't look at ourselves like we are the s**t. We allow the material success to outshine our internal growth. We place little value on the path we have travelled to get where we are. Many of us have achieved our dreams for the simple fact we have overcome and reached the place we're at. Just because there may not be the lifestyle or the financial success, that shouldn't take away from the fact we have achieved what we once thought was impossible.

"I've come too far now to not express who I am. I've lived in the shadow of myself for too long, I stepped out of the darkness and since that day I have not looked back."

ACHIEVABLE WAYS OF LIVING

You see when you purposely compensate your own character and energy for the purpose of allowing others to shine, you give yourself reason to question your worth. When you possess a powerful aura and a contagious energy, it can cause people to envy you for the simple fact you are empowering and possess something they fail to see within themselves.

This doesn't mean you are to shy away from who you are just so you don't hurt other people's feelings. That's their own insecurities they must learn to manage and deal with. You...you must shine, and shine bright. Ensure to protect your energy and be intelligent enough to know how and when to shine your brightest. As good and as pure as your heart may be, someone, somewhere is praying on your downfall. It's harsh and sounds extreme but it's reality. It's important to be aware of the energy you are surrounded by.

"This is the start of something extraordinary. I am going to transform my life and the lives of others. The scale of growth I am looking to generate is far beyond anything I have previously experienced. It is about mind, body and spirit. Living and creating a lifestyle built of love, experience, connection, integrity, honesty and courage. I strictly refuse to place myself amongst the ungrateful. I have made a conscious decision to place myself in a position of truth. I intend on remaining as close to my own character as I can. Although I value my words, the real truth comes from my actions."

"I am a person who expresses my intentions through my behaviour. I must live free. What doesn't sit right with my soul, I have no interest in entertaining. My life is not supposed to be played safe or getting by on auto pilot. It's about taking risks, expressing my rawness and putting everything that I am, into my dreams. I wish and hope for nothing as I have full faith and determination. What comes and happens is supposed to and is in the hands of a factor beyond my intelligence. Here's to the pure and clean-hearted, go out into the world and experience your greatness."

ACHIEVABLE WAYS OF LIVING

CHAPTER 2:

I'M IN THE PURSUIT OF
GREATNESS...

"Success waits for no man. This isn't a game where you pick and choose when to work hard. This journey has to be a commitment. You've got to be prepared to give the best you can, when and where you can."

ACHIEVABLE WAYS OF LIVING

It's that deep, you can't afford to go at your dream half hearted. Life is too hard to be living at less than what you are capable of. You've got to double down to get yourself in a position where your greatness is able to flourish.

Study any highly successful person and see the extent of their commitment. The higher their success, the deeper their commitment travels. I challenge you to commit to yourself for one whole month, experience what comes when you sacrifice and go all in for what you want. You will be amazed at the result you generate from being committed and consistent. Go ahead and go for it.

Remember...you either win or you learn.

"To fulfil your dreams, you can't operate normally. There is a complete shift in mindset and lifestyle. No way can you expect to act common and get an uncommon outcome. This s**t is different. The journey is nothing like you have experienced before and if you are not prepared to withstand the struggles or the work ethic required, reconsider your ambitions."

ACHIEVABLE WAYS OF LIVING

This is a whole new approach to life. When you've got something you believe in down to the core of your heart...when it's all you think about, talk about and be about, it's impossible to live a normal everyday life. A dream is a lifetime commitment and not everyone has the endurance to see it through. There is a small percentage of this world who are out doing what is at the centre of their soul. Are you going to be part of that percentage?

"If you are inconsistent, you can kiss goodbye to whatever you are trying to pursue. To be able to show up everyday and do something that brings you closer to your goal is an achievement within itself, more so, on the days you are less motivated and least interested. It's what you do on those days that count. If you can get it on the days you don't feel up to it, you're winning. Consistency is key."

ACHIEVABLE WAYS OF LIVING

How bad do you want it on the days you don't feel like it? That is a powerful way to measure your determination. It's not even about turning up and going all in. It is about showing up and giving it all that you have on that day. You are not always going to be 100% up for it. Some days you are going to consider giving it in and calling it a day.

I want you to feel like s**t, and then I want you to get it while you feel like s**t, so you can get a real taste of what it feels like to see yourself act against your own mood. You learn to do this, you'll see why so many other things are possible from life when you are consistent and you turn up. The longer the snowball rolls, the faster, stronger and bigger it becomes.

"You must understand that all skills are learnable. To improve a skill requires practice and to practice requires effort. Therefore, the more effort that is put into practice, the more improved you are going to be at performing that skill."

ACHIEVABLE WAYS OF LIVING

Take a moment to look at those who you admire. Use them as your inspiration. Use them as your motivation. And just know that, whatever you desire — it is possible. However, it is imperative to understand that when you decide to pursue something new or outside your comfort zone, you will not be as good as the person you are trying to emulate. This is factor you must accept.

Over time with an insane work ethic, border line obession and a dedication to relentlessly strive to improve, you will come to see yourself reaching the targets you set out to reach. Whatever it may be that you are aspiring to, learn what it takes to get it, go out there and make it happen. You've got this.

"You can be as good as the degree you decide to work."

ACHIEVABLE WAYS OF LIVING

The opportunity is there for us all. It's a matter of willingness to put in the effort to stretch and push yourself to be the best you can be.

With a high work ethic comes high rewards. If you can aim to outwork yourself and be open to remaining a student of your field, you will come to realise it's only the amount of effort which is holding you back at any stage. The ownership is on you.

"Make use of your talents. Share with the world what you are good at. Life credits those who utilise their abilities."

ACHIEVABLE WAYS OF LIVING

We all have a divine talent or a set of skills that is beyond the ordinary. These may not be at the level of an elite performer but there is a skill there within us all. This skill may be a way of connecting with people, how you intake and share information; an intellectual skill rather than a more noticable, physical one.

What counts is how much effort, time and energy gets invested into developing your unique ability. If you can work on yourself enough to the point where you are recognised for the level of your talent you will find opportunities beginning to appear. If you continue to work relentlessly, your skills will soon be able to pay the bills.

"Opportunities are presented often but it takes a trained eye to see the value. Don't miss out on the solution by using too much energy to focus on the problem."

ACHIEVABLE WAYS OF LIVING

It helps to know what you are looking for. A trained eye is developed through clarity. When you can operate with a clear vision of what you are aiming for, you pay more attention to the detail of what you are focusing on. Therefore, you are more likely to see it when it crosses your path.

When you pour too much energy into the problem, it blinds you from opportunities surrounding the solution. Use your focus wisely and in the process you will be training yourself to become a more 'solution based' thinker, rather than just being locked into the depth of the problem.

"Feeding the mind with materials that enhance your vision and strengthen your beliefs, is something to most certainly consider."

ACHIEVABLE WAYS OF LIVING

There are tremendous benefits when the mind is nourished. An idle mind left to operate independently spells danger. Not just that, we have at our disposal one of, if not the most fascinating and wonderful tool known to mankind.

Our mind.

Look into what human beings have created! All is the result of an inspired mind. Use your imagination to your advantage and you may just be surpised at what you have the ability to produce or create.

"Obsession is the driving force which fuels and inspires greatness. An intense interest in one's chosen field is what will separate the common from the uncommon."

ACHIEVABLE WAYS OF LIVING

Look at some of the world's greatest athletes. Listen to their language, observe their work ethic and you will begin to see why they are at the peak of their game. They are in a domain where competition is high and there are thousands of others who have a desire to be the best, yet only those small few excel.

Why is that? What is the difference?
The hunger to keep learning, the emotional connection and continuous growing interest. Creating a healthy obsession is essential if there is any ambition to be great.

"Driven by passion, governed by a force with no breaks. It moves at such speed that doubt just can not keep up. It carries so much faith that fear doesn't even stand a chance."

ACHIEVABLE WAYS OF LIVING

The mindset of a champion...when you surrender to the journey and everything that comes with it, there's a force which activates at the core of your soul; a higher version of yourself rises to the surface and ferociously attacks each and every one of your goals.

This higher version of yourself sees no excuse, nor does it back down from any challenge. It is extremely focused, determined and relentless. Only through letting go of who you are and sacrificing to this version of yourself, are you able to activate the champion within.

"It is better to stand alone than it is to follow the crowd that is criticising the man alone."

ACHIEVABLE WAYS OF LIVING

This is for those who refuse to confine, who don't fit into society's image. To the creative's and the visionaries who are regularly misunderstood. Continue to keep blazing your path, you will meet others along the way who appreciate the uniqueness and the quality you display.

Keep creating and expressing yourself in your unique fashion, be it through the way you dress, draw, speak, dance... who cares? Be you! You are an outcast, made to stand out in the way you do. You weren't born to fit in and you should have no reason to want to. You are the creator of your reality, an inspiration of the highest kind. Shine bright and don't let the world dim your light!

I want to express and share with you my definition of success. Throughout my writing, you will see a lot of talk related to accomplishment and success. Personally speaking my success is 90% connected to my internal growth, if I can overcome the voice of doubt and take action upon my goals — that right there is my success.

My relationship with myself is my most valuable accomplishment. Although I may not have the materials which may reflect success. I can confidently say I am successful. This is about a feeling, a freedom within myself to know that what I've accomplished within myself exceeds finanical value. To have come from an internally dark place to then learn how to create light, I promise you there is nothing like it.

To live with self-doubt and negative thoughts to then feel and live with confidence and empowerment I can only smile as words do the feeling little justice. When you are content within yourself, you long for nothing other than more of the same feeling. You find yourself acting in a way you've always visioned, there is an overwhelming feeling of gratitude as something at the core of you has always wanted this. There is nothing which comes close to it.

You feel unstoppable, you have the belief to overcome and the faith to do what once seemed literally impossible. Throughout history, it has been proven that when you walk with the right attitude, which you will soon see for yourself, you achieve whatever you set you mind to.

ACHIEVABLE WAYS OF LIVING

The stuggle which comes with life is nothing compared to the faith which comes from belief. The way I perceive life, my beliefs, my impact on others is how I measure my success. I'm not quite sure if in societies eyes this is worth celebrating but to me, this is my everything.

Being content within yourself is the essence of living. Feeling comfortable in your own skin and not feeling any less of a human being than somebody who is material or financially rich is the ultimate bag. My advice to you all is to learn how to acquire self-assurance. Manage your ego and insecurities through analysing and regualry re-evaluating what you value and stand for. The only external success I measure is the impact and influence I have upon people. I put a lot of focus into my contribution to others. It helps keep me grounded and I believe service is the greatest gift one can give. With those two elements tied to my success, I live in a peaceful and ever growing space.

There is no real reason for me to live in a place of comparison or to feel any less successful than the person who has just purchased the lastest supercar, as we both may evaluate and measure our success of different metrics. With that being said, I now offer you the opportunity to go within yourself and evaluate how you measure your success? What does success mean to you? How will you know when you are successful?

What is your definition of success?
Explain what success means to you...

_____

_____

_____

_____

_____

_____

_____

_____

_____

_____

_____

_____

_____

ACHIEVABLE WAYS OF LIVING

CHAPTER 3:

BY DOING WHAT'S DIFFICULT...

"This journey of personal development and growth is such a turbulant experience.
You can reach the heights of new found happiness and the lows of past experiences. To be sure the journey continues in an upward spiral you've got to be consistent with your understanding and persistent with your efforts towards daily growth. You will question, doubt and have thoughts of wanting to give up but with those feelings you will have a little voice inside of you that is bursting with energy and fuelling you with positivity to keep the journey going."

ACHIEVABLE WAYS OF LIVING

Inspiration can be deceiving.
It's easy to mistake inspiration for entertainment. Just because it is inspiring doesn't mean it is easy or fun.

The journey of personal development is life changing but it is strenuous and requires sheer determination and patience. Be careful, because if you're not, inspiration will pull wool over your eyes and have life smack you right in the face.

It takes courage to stick to the path of turning yourself inside out and dealing with the wave of emotions that comes with self-improvement. As daunting as it may sound, the rewards far outweigh the difficulties that come with personal development.

"We all have a limit. After we've realised that, we then have a choice to either exceed that limit or remain under it. If we choose to remain under it we will forever have a limit. If we choose to exceed that limit, progress to exceed the next limit and keep that momentum going, we will soon begin to see we are in fact actually almost limitless."

ACHIEVABLE WAYS OF LIVING

If you are not willing to go beyond the edge of your limits, your skills will be capped at a level that is enough to keep you content, but not enough to keep you hungry.

As long as there is always something to learn, there is always going to be room to grow. The more you grow, the more you begin to see yourself in a positive way.

"There is no better way, than to learn through experience. To f**k up, fail or take a risk that doesn't pay off. The greatest lessons remain hidden within failure and adversity."

ACHIEVABLE WAYS OF LIVING

It all happens through doing. The theoretical aspect is excellent and does serve its purpose, but it doesn't provide the same stimulus or knowledge that getting a first hand feel would.

With partaking in experience you instantly receive live feedback. You can, in the moment, reflect and come up with a way of how to improve your efforts.

Action is the antidote. To do is to learn and to learn is to do. You want to see how it will plan out? Take action and learn from the experiences.

"If you are doubting yourself, you are going in the right direction. If you are pursuing something and it is causing you to question your capabilities... BINGO! That's exactly what you should be pursuing. If it scares you, it's perfect for you."

ACHIEVABLE WAYS OF LIVING

You learn very little remaining in an area you excel in, although there are extremely amazing benefits of repetition and reinforcement. There are very little feelings as powerful as overcoming doubt.

Understand the development phase. The fundamentals always remain the same, it's just the challenge which varies. It goes a lot like this...doubt and do, or doubt and don't do. When you doubt and do, you learn and you develop a new belief and with that, you feel more secure within yourself to make another attempt, only this time backed with more knowledge confidence and reassurance.

This is repeated until the once doubtful task becomes a skill. When you doubt and don't do, you are left with the thought that you are inferior and incapable of progressing in that area. If not careful, this is a belief which can spread and travel into other areas of your life.

"You mustn't be afraid
to face the pain of feeling
uncomfortable when trying
something new."

ACHIEVABLE WAYS OF LIVING

Nobody is an expert after their first attempt of trying something new. This applies to any situation where you feel uncomfortable with your current skills and abilities. Embarking on a new venture does require a mindset that is prepared to persist through the barriers and mental blocks. One must be willing to learn and be open as the early stages can be quite strenuous.

Yes, it hurts when we fail and our lack of skills are exposed to a wider audience or we are not up to the standards of others. That's okay, as with time and effort, progress arises. Do not let your lack of knowledge dishearten you or allow a poor performance crush your self-esteem.

Remember, nobody starts as an expert. As long as you are willing to learn, the performances will come. Once you begin to improve, you will see it's a build up, an accumulation of hours spent improving on the present task.

"We've got to be prepared
to go beyond uncomfortable. If big
dreams are what we say we want,
then big action is what we
must take."

ACHIEVABLE WAYS OF LIVING

This is the price to pay. Uncomfortable becomes the new norm. The journey can be a daunting one when you are coming from an ordinary background with limited opportunies and you are not familiar with travelling too far outside your comfrot zone, but hey... there is no time to play victim. This is our situation and not much is going to change unless we do something about it, so let's buckle up and hit the road. What's the next big action you can take that will bring you a step closer to your dream?

"The majority of people are too lazy to go the extra mile. If you put in the kind of effort that exceeds the average attempt, over a period of time you are going to reach a place far beyond where society would consider possible to reach, giving you much more of an upper hand in moving forward."

ACHIEVABLE WAYS OF LIVING

Think...over the course of a year, if you were to put in an extra hour every day that you work...at the end of the year, you would have accumulated an extra _____ hours on top of what you have already done.

Combined with an analytical approach and intention based practice, by the end of the year, the results would be evident. This is the difference between those who excel exceptionally and those who maintain the same level of performance.

"Seek a vocation that reflects who you are as a person. An occupation that is a representation of your character, a direct alignment of your morals. Does such a vocation exist? Not until you go out and discover it!"

ACHIEVABLE WAYS OF LIVING

'How do you find your passion?' We don't find it, we create it. Our passion is a combination of our experiences, our interests and our skills. What we've previously done in our past that has brought us fulfilment, along with where our skills and interests lie.

It can be soul destroying working in a job or being stuck in a career path you have zero to little interest in. Should you go out there, gamble it all and become an entreprenuer? No! You've got to go out into the world and discover within yourself what you enjoy.

I know things are a lot easier said than done. Does it come with its difficulties? Of course it does. Does it come with risk and uncertainty? Absolutely. It also comes with opportunity, not only to find a new occupation but to grow as an indvidual. Life is about experience and getting the most value out of our time. Do you really want to waste time being stuck in a position you have no real desire or love to be in?

"Whilst chasing your dream,
be it building a brand or business, you
have to be prepared to face the days
of darkness. The days when it seems
like nobody is believing in what you're
doing. When you start to question
yourself and the journey, it's in these
times you have to be firm and stand
by your belief because without belief,
there is no dream."

ACHIEVABLE WAYS OF LIVING

The day comes. It comes fast and it comes often. Persisting is hard and it requires a lot of mental strength but it's necessary. If something deep within you is not gravitating you towards materialising your vision, it is very unlikely you will withstand the pressure that comes with actualising your goals.

Commitment is non-negotiable. Not just the word commitment but the actions and everything the word stands for. The late nights, the sacrifices, the planning, the tedious tasks, the discipline to choose top priority duties. If you can find the courage and the spirit to stick by yourself in the times of darkness and confusion, slowly you will see not only your efforts but your self-esteem rewarded.

"The world has already formed its opinion of you so there isn't much point trying to prove to people who you are. The best way to alter other peoples opinions of you is to live your truth. Operate freely, allow other people to correct themselves, let others challenge and change their own opinion through you being who you are with rawness and integrity. You only strengthen their opinion the more you try and prove them wrong."

ACHIEVABLE WAYS OF LIVING

Human beings are visual animals. It is our first form of contact. We are heavily influenced by what we see. If a lion were to approach you with blood dripping from its mouth, you would believe this lion is dangerous and will definitely attack you.

Same applies for our image.

People judge through what they see. Our character is what shatters people's opinion, when how we act goes against what they believe. If that same lion were to approach you and start to lick and play with you, it would dramatically change your belief and opinion of that particular lion.

"Be real to yourself.
Knowing you are being genuine towards whatever cause you are committed to is empowering. People may not acknowledge your authenticity, and you may not even get the appreciation that you deserve, but that shouldn't ever stop you being true to you."

ACHIEVABLE WAYS OF LIVING

How do you feel about *you* when you are by yourself? Are you able to hold yourself accountable for the goals you set? Do you have the integrity to be honest and truthful in times you least feel like admitting and facing the fact you've f***ked up?

This, for me, is essential as it's not as if anybody will know any different whether you do or don't, but *you* will. You are always watching you. Failing to be honest with ourselves affects self-worth. A lack of trust begins to develop which causes a feeling of disconnection.

Although some can live through life ignoring the dysfunctional relationship they have with themselves, for you, this is a top priority and you should always take the route of being true to you. Always take the opportunity to strengthen the relationship you have with yourself at any given opportunity.

In case you are wondering why I frequently write about dreams, ambitions and mindset I've come from a place where this world was once non-existent. I've come from a single parent household, council estate, working-class background. I've witnessed my mother climb mountains and overcome debt and adversity on several occasions. This was my norm. And I'm sure when I'm speaking here, there are many who can relate. When you're young, seeing your parent/parents struggle and work unhealthy hours at multiple jobs just to keep your head above the water changes the way you view the world.

Growing up in a city with little to no expectations, surrounded by drug addicts, prostitutes, criminals and people with no aspirations, it affects you subconsciously and you grow up confused. As you mature, you start seeing reality for what it is which slowly starts to zap your spirit. You see it's a trap, a system designed to keep you supressed. How is somebody with no positive influences supposed to make it out of such a setup independently? I was fortunate to have a mother and mentor who believed I would someday grow up to make something of myself. The same can not be said for many other young people who are living under the same circumstances, it's a struggle and it still haunts me. Aren't we supposed to live with expression and creativty? Aren't we supposed to be able explore our dreams and ideas instead of dealing with difficulty from an early age, focused to become a product of our environment through no fault of our own. It's a personal mission for me to inspire, to share that there is more to life and we don't have to settle for what the system has trapped us in. There is a way out and I'm walking that path and sharing every step along the way.

It's rare that people within the 'working class' socio-economic background go against the norm and do something out of the ordinary — I've done exactly that. Once I got a taste of this mindset and this other side to life, there was no going back. This is how it is supposed to be. The same system that kills dreams, tames creative spirits and keeps the inspired trapped and supressed. I carved my way out, the fear of ever having to go back to that lifestyle drives me to improve myself and society every breathing moment of my life. I cannot live to accept mediocracy, I'm reshuffling the cards life dealt me with and coming back to the table with a stronger hand.

I've had to over-obsess, as I see it as a once in a lifetime opportunity to create for myself and my family. If I can work hard enough and make use of my skills, I'll be able to live life knowing I stood up and followed my dreams despite my starting point. I am courageous enough to walk the path of the unknown. I aim to create for myself and my family a lifestyle that will enable my children to grow in a creative and inspiring environment. This is why I learn about the mindset of dreamers, visionaries and creatives. For me, this is my survival mechanism. I can either settle and remain a product of my environment or I can rise and do what it takes to change the course of my life forever. This is a do or die situation, life is a constant battle, we have to turn up everyday and give it the best we can when we can. This takes priming the mind to think positively about the battles we face, keeping our thoughts clear and feeding our mind with reasons to believe that there's more to life and our dreams are possible.

Define your 'Why'...*(Describe in detail)*

_____

_____

_____

_____

_____

_____

_____

_____

_____

_____

_____

_____

_____

ACHIEVABLE WAYS OF LIVING

"Your why is your driving force. The reason you refuse to give in when adversity comes knocking."

_____

_____

_____

_____

_____

_____

_____

_____

_____

_____

_____

_____

_____

BREATE:

Give yourself a moment.

Inhale with the least ammount of effort and then exhale freely. Experience, allow yourself to be.

With every exhale you become lighter and lighter

Close your eyes and for as long as you feel necessary contiune to breathe freely and lightly

When you are done, smile and pick up where you left off...

ACHIEVABLE WAYS OF LIVING

I have to say so far this experience has been life changing. The difficulty that comes with creating a body of work that you aim to inspire and change lives with is an extremely challenging path to travel. Writing in a note pad is calm, there's no pressure attached to it but creating something for the public is a whole new ball game. You have to live in the thoughts of your target audience, feel what they are feeling, think what they may be thinking and then create a universal message. This should resonate enough to deliver reassurance and provide the reader with exactly the message of inspiration that they're looking for.

Writing so consistently over the length of time it has taken me to publish this book has transformed me. It's exposed me to my weaknesses. I've learnt more about myself during the creation of this book than I have through any other method of writing. I've realised that through writing, I tap into my 'flow' state. I zone in and reality disappears. It's just me, the page and the thoughts of the reader. I believe I have discovered what it means to experience and live your passion.

I'm glad I made the decision to publish a book. As tedious and frustrating as the journey has been, I'm proud I have created a piece of work that will outlive me. I can now say I am that friend you can always rely on. Whether I am dead or alive, my energy and message is here to stay — mission accomplished!

One final note before we move on. Although I am curious to see how far and wide this book will travel, my only honest ambitions are for it to land in the hands of those who need it the most.

CHAPTER 4:

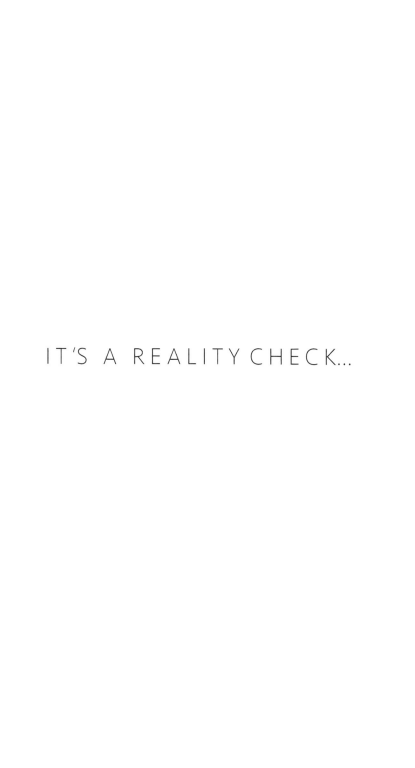

IT'S A REALITY CHECK...

"Life isn't about waiting for the right opportunity, it's about taking the opportunity at any time and making it right."

ACHIEVABLE WAYS OF LIVING

Will the time ever be right? Even if I fall victim to the fear of waiting for the right moment. There is a slight truth in it but it's not to the level of procrastination we can sometimes take it to. It's like the more you take the opportunity when you're not ready, the harder the reality hits home of "I should have done this a long time ago. Why did I wait so long?" Not being ready can sometimes be more beneficial than actually being ready.

There's a difference between taking a risk and taking a calculated risk. A risk is a blind action going against unfavourable odds. Whereas a calculated risk is more secure as all scenarios have been taken into account beforehand. If you are ever considering on whether to take the risk or not, rather than just running forward aimlessly or not taking any action at all, weigh up the benefits and disadvantages and move forward with what you believe is more suitable for you.

"If you want things to improve and get better, you get better. If you want things to grow, you grow. We have the ability to influence and control life to a certain degree, but if we are unaware of that ability and fail to use it, we quickly become a product of what life makes us,
rather than what we make us."

ACHIEVABLE WAYS OF LIVING

The power is within us all. We cannot choose what life decides to present us with, but we can choose how we react and what we do with what life gives us. It's a shame to see how many people go through life with little to no control over their situation when they have it within them to redirect their ship.

Take this knowledge with you into your next challenge and see what results you get from standing up to life and taking ownership. Refuse to give in to the situation. You are not the victim. You are the survivor, the warrior who takes the troops to war, not the commander who signals the flag of surrender.

"You've got to face your problems. As much as they may take you back, the strength of facing them moves you forward."

ACHIEVABLE WAYS OF LIVING

Too right it's scary. You will be taken back when facing your problems. You have to confront your insecurities head on but hey...if you want self-improvement, it's about approaching life with a little steel in your character. Never will you hear me say 'it's easy', no way! I don't even believe it gets easier. The more we do it, I just think the more tolerant and understanding we become of what it takes.

'You can' and 'you will.' That is all that matters. You will be amazed at how many people don't actually face their issues. So to know that you are, is extra motivation for you. You are doing what's necessary and important. I praise you for your courage and determination. I've felt what it's like to look yourself in the mirror and not be happy with what you see. To face your trauma isn't pretty under any circumstance, especially to do so voluntarily...it's not for the faint-hearted. Once again, I praise you and pray you continue to display the strength of character which has seen you reach this far.

"You can't see the beauty of the present whilst looking at the ugliness of the past."

ACHIEVABLE WAYS OF LIVING

You can't look in two different directions at the same time. I invite you to look around you, pause for a moment, soak it in...how much has changed? How much have you grown as a person? What do you have in your life, which at one stage, was only a wish, a hope? What's different about your 'now' compared to your 'then?'

You are no longer the person you were, that person didn't know what you know now. You are new. Allow yourself to stop looking at yourself through a broken lens. It's time you started taking ownership and appreciating the journey you've travelled. You have permission to look back, only to see the distance you've travelled. For any other reason, you have no permission. Today is your focus. You've carried the weight for too long. Drop it and leave it where it is. Right now, as your life is at it is. How much good do you have around you? That's it, fix your focus on that question and move forward gracefully.

"We can get so caught up in trying to live up to other people's expectations of us, that we end up living through their perceptions of us rather than how we perceive ourselves."

ACHIEVABLE WAYS OF LIVING

In the politest way this can come across, f**k them. Live you. We have to remind ourselves of our greatness and our individuality daily. Whenever you find yourself slipping into the thought of how others perceive you, revert back to this page and remind yourself of why it is important to set your own expectations.

What people say about you holds as much weight as you give it. Remember that if you give it no energy, it holds no power.

"If nothing within you changes, nothing outside of you changes. If you would like to witness magic, change the way you think and watch the world shift right before your eyes."

ACHIEVABLE WAYS OF LIVING

Our minds are fixated on what we already know. Each individual's perspective, thoughts and beliefs have been shaped and conditioned unconsciously due to what each individual has been exposed to or surrounded by. Until we do not take the initative to consciously begin changing our thoughts and perspectives, we will forever see the world in the same pattern we have always witnessed it.

There are many ways in which one can view the world. Only when we allow ourselves to see different, can we experience different. Perception is reality. Change your perspective — change your reality.

"Know when your words are to be
muted and your actions are
to be put on loud."

ACHIEVABLE WAYS OF LIVING

We all reach a stage where there is not much else left to say, other than what we show. Our words only hold power for a short period of time before our actions have to align with what we are saying.

Otherwise, we'll fall into the category of a person of many words but little action...a wishful thinker, even worse...a liar. If you can say what you do, and do what you say, you haven't got to worry.

Our actions are the clear indication of our intentions...not our words.

What is the purpose of life if you are afraid to live and also afraid to die?

ACHIEVABLE WAYS OF LIVING

What is your purpose if that is the case? You remain trapped by the fear of living your life to the best of your ability and you are terrified at the thought of facing death.

So, what is it you are actually doing with your one opportunity in this physical realm? Live it up! Nature is always going to be at work, so don't let your thoughts stop you from grabbing one hell of an experience whilst you have this golden opportunity called *'Life'*.

"If you are not getting the results you want from the current way you are operating, do you not think a change in approach will help?"

ACHIEVABLE WAYS OF LIVING

Albert Einstein once said *"Insanity is doing the same thing over and over again and expecting different results".* Ignoring the signs needed to improve can result in one developing cognitive dissonance — the inability to take in new information which will enable you to make much needed changes. Our ignorance can quickly become our blindfold, clouding our ability to assess our ineffective working habits.

There is no harm in taking a different approach and being open to change. Purposely take on board new ideas and seek constructive criticism. Humble pie doesn't taste as bad as you may think it does; it's actually quite healthy for you. All jokes aside, sometimes our vision can be limited, we need other perspectives to compensate for our blind spots.

"Telling somebody to believe in themselves isn't enough. Motivation is good for the moment but people learn the most through experience. Seeing the result of one's efforts is what gives us the belief. Seeing ourselves improve is what gives us the inspiration to believe in ourselves. Self-belief... the word 'self' is important because that's the only place where the belief from within can come from...ourselves. People may empower us and motivate us but the bottom line is, it takes us to believe in us."

ACHIEVABLE WAYS OF LIVING

Placing too much reliance on people hinders the authority and respect we have for ourselves. As good as it is hearing people speak to us in an empowering way, their words will only carry us so far. A tip for us all to remember is that when we are sharing a message, the message has much more of an impact when conveyed through our behaviour than it ever will through our words.Seeing will have more of an impact than speaking ever will.

"Tell me and I'll forget, show me and I might remember, involve me and I will understand"
- Chinese Proverb.

"The way I see it is...when I look back at my life I want to be able to smile at all the risks I've taken, regardless of all the odds that were stacked against me. I want to see that I followed what I believed in."

ACHIEVABLE WAYS OF LIVING

What more is there to it? Isn't that the ultimate form of satisfaction. Being able to look back upon your life and be internally fulfilled that you lived it according to your beliefs?

You refused to live in the fear of other people's thoughts and was prepared to face the criticism. You stood by what you felt was right, despite others telling you otherwise. That, right there, is what self-satisfaction is all about.

Write in great detail about what you are most
grateful for in your life? Why?

_____

_____

_____

_____

_____

_____

_____

_____

_____

_____

_____

_____

_____

CHAPTER 5:

BECAUSE IN THE EYE'S OF
THE UNIVERSE...

"A lot can happen within a year. Life is a constant motion of change. Life is constantly evolving and we too must adapt and change with life. A year from now a whole lot will be different. Circumstances change daily, new paths get crossed and new opportunities arise. One's life is rarely ever the same. This current situation you are in right now is just a moment in a long journey. The feelings are temporary, so try not get too comfortable or overwhelmed. Pay attention and you will begin to see a common theme: adapt and grow."

ACHIEVABLE WAYS OF LIVING

Everything is temporary. All we can do is adapt — be the situation positive or negative. The goal is to figure out how we can use our experiences to propel us forward. Sometimes we can find ourselves trapped in the thought of complacency and expecting things to continue in the manner in which they are or this situation is never going to end.

Things do come to an end and new beginnings arise. Even if the situation is extremely positive, it soon changes. The key is to enjoy life, be present and to learn. One cannot be defeated nor disheartened with this type of attitude.

"It is not the strongest of the species that survive, nor the most intelligent, but the one most responsive to change".
Charles Darwin

"It is hard saying 'things happen for a reason' when you are going through the happening. But they do. They also happen at the time they are supposed to happen. Why? That is beyond my understanding or control. One thing I do know is that the reason why they happen always serves a purpose."

ACHIEVABLE WAYS OF LIVING

It's time to get a little philosophical. If it wasn't supposed to happen, why would it happen? It's hard not to believe in a force more powerful than human beings when life plays out like our paths are already pre-written. Reflect upon everything you have experienced to this present day. Look at how it has led you to this present moment. When you think about it, each moment has served a purpose. Each moment is exactly what and how it is supposed to be.

"Time moves slowly.
Creeping from one day to another,
sometimes without us even
noticing. Staying present can be a
difficult task as our lives are
constantly on the go. Our best bet is
to take charge of each of our
mornings and plan in advance for
the days ahead. This stops us from
living life on auto pilot and keeps us
conscious of our lives from
day to day."

ACHIEVABLE WAYS OF LIVING

Life happens.

Before you've even realised, months have passed and you haven't yet even achieved half of what you've set for yourself. Very little quality time has been spent with friends and family. It's done unintentionally as we live passively and get complacent with the expectation of tomorrow.

But tomorrow isn't promised.

Although the chances of seeing tomorrow are high, it helps to always have a sense of urgency when it comes to pursuing our dreams and fulfilling our duties.

"Your time will come. You will arrive where you belong, you will be with who is right for you. In the meantime, do what you have to do."

ACHIEVABLE WAYS OF LIVING

It's all in the script of life. Faith is the ingredient. Create a long term vision. None of us come out of life alive, so whilst we are here, is it worth stressing over areas we have little control over? I think not.

Our focus should be glued to elements of life we are able to control. The best thing you can do for yourself is to keep going and do what you can with what you've got. Trust how your life is unfolding. Rarely does life put us in positions without something valuable to draw from it. There is always something to gain...always! It may not be something you learn right away but over due time, the writing will soon be on the wall.

"If you can learn how to forgive, you will experience a life of freedom. When you let go of hatred towards others, you enter a world of serenity and empathy. It is more beneficial for your mental health to forgive than it is to hold any form of hatred or ideas of revenge."

ACHIEVABLE WAYS OF LIVING

I'll be the first to tell you it isn't easy. People hurt us and will continue to betray and disrespect us and yes, it does take time to heal. That's natural but the manner in which we choose to heal, and what we do whilst we heal, plays a huge part in our development and attitude in moving forward.

Cleanse your soul by letting go of the toxic energy that is attracted to negativity and hatred. Forgive and allow your spirit to heal in peace. Life will serve those with bad nature. You keep your focus on what's important and what's going to help you become a better person.

"There are many lessons humans can learn from plants. The lesson I am referring to here is that when a plant loses a leaf, it has no time to dwell or ask questions. It simply starts reproducing another leaf. The fallen leaf has paved the way for another to come to life. Humans should apply the same philosophy to people and to opportunities."

ACHIEVABLE WAYS OF LIVING

Life is a factor which is always at work. Mother nature doesn't stop. Animals have zero time to feel remorse as survival and reproduction is their only priority.

In life, losses are inevitable. Let's face facts for a moment and accept that our physical existence is temporary. The same applies for opportunities and connections. Leaves fall due to the season, they have served their purpose and it's time for new leaves to serve theirs and the cycle continues.

Not everybody who enters our lives are supposed to remain. Learning to continue with life is a harsh truth which we have to accept. In order for our species to continue evolving, we have to keep following the course of mother nature.

"Social friends come and go but soul mates... soul mates last forever."

ACHIEVABLE WAYS OF LIVING

Once two souls align and connect, it is very rare those souls will ever part. Regardless of the time spent apart or the distance, true connection will always remain. In a way beyond my intelligence, time apart strengthens true bonds.

It's up to you to identify who's in your life for the long term and who's in your life just for a temporary period. Social friends will come, play their role for as long as needed, after that, there is little left to build from and time will see them depart.
For soul mates, the relationship seems to grow from strength to strength. Time is an ultimate indication of a relationship, it either strenghtens or it weakens. Pay attention to the relationships that time strengthens.

"As educators we are to provide zero answers, in a sense, we are to switch roles and become the student. Giving our pupils the independence to seek the answer of their own initative."

ACHIEVABLE WAYS OF LIVING

As role models, leaders, coaches and people in a position of influence, it is vital that we step back from providing those we serve with the answers. Our teaching should encourage independent thinking, allowing our students to go out into the world and find the answers through their own experiences.

What good is it if all we do is teach the lesson and share the answer? The aim is for students to rely upon themselves to ask the question and seek the answer. The whole idea of them depending on us for answers should be eradicated. We are only to probe, show the way and present problems for them to solve. What counts is not how much they learn when you are around but how well they perform when they are no longer your students.

"It is always good to take a well-deserved break from social media, especially if you are a high profile figure or a person who receives more than the average attention. Our confidence and self-esteem can be easily tied to a social media platform. It is easy to be seduced by the immediate attention that is given at the click of a button. The false affection you receive has the power to lead you astray, far beyond the reach of your true self."

ACHIEVABLE WAYS OF LIVING

Remember the attention we receive on social media platforms serves little purpose compared to the attention we receive in reality. It is easy to get wrapped up in the image we portray of ourselves and the positive feedback we receive on our social platforms.

By no means am I taking away the benefits nor saying all that we see online is fake; the statistics and evidence speak for itself. But the pressure to live up to an image can increasingly become overwhelming and people have fast become lost in the game of portraying the perfect lifestyle.

I'm sure you are aware and doing what you can to keep your distance and using your platfrom as a way to share positivity. This is just a reminder to be mindful of the dangers that are connected to social media. Look after your mental health by keeping a safe distance and using it for the socialising tool that it is.

"There are opportunities out in the universe. There are opportunities awaiting your arrival but if you do not walk the path, if you do not run in the direction of openings, what chance will you have?"

ACHIEVABLE WAYS OF LIVING

There is opportunity out there, but without us even stepping foot into the vast pool of what is awaiting us, we will never experience what more there is to offer. The moment we decided to act is the moment we activate the laws of the universe.

When we hesitate or over-analyse, it only causes procrastination and further spirals us deeper into inaction and doubt.

"Too often we mistake our reality for just what we can physically see. We become blinded by what's in front of us. Seldom do we look within, it's there where the beauty of life lays. To see what's not, is to see what is."

ACHIEVABLE WAYS OF LIVING

The world within us is extraordinary. It's the place where our visions, our imagination and our dreams live. There is room to think creatively. Our ideas have permission to roam free. It is fascinating how wonderful this place is, yet alarming how many people rarely choose to explore it as they choose to entertain external influences instead.

Connecting with our inner-self positively affects our reality. Thoughts can become things. We have the ability to manifest what we see through execution, planning and preparation. Your dreams are not just dreams but an extension of 'you' waiting to be manifested.

"It happens but you've got to give it time. The healing, the breakthrough, the success. It all comes but only to those who are patient enough to stick by long enough to see it materialise. There is no shortcut. You've got it in you to endure the process."

ACHIEVABLE WAYS OF LIVING

You've seen it prevail before and the good news is you will see it prevail again. The bad news is you've got to go through the suffering, questioning, doubting and the days of feeling like s**t. If there was a way to skip the process, I'm sure the world would know about it, as of yet, pain is the way.

"When you think about it, negatives are actually positives. Positives are in a sense, deceiving, as everything is flowing, everything is going right, it can quickly become passive. There isn't much intense learning going on. Whereas with a negative experience, everything comes to life. The moment gets your full attention. I think negatives are highly misunderstood for the potential they possess."

ACHIEVABLE WAYS OF LIVING

DIAMOND IN THE DIRT

It's not that we are not to enjoy our positive experiences or to fully embrace the time when things are going well...but rather to understand it is not all as bad as it seems when things are going wrong.

When things are going wrong, it is the perfect opportunity to learn a valuable lesson or two about ourselves. It is a chance for our flaws to be exposed and for us to see how strong we are. Engage with your negatives in order to fully appreciate your positives.

"Peace of mind or happiness? Personally, I choose peace of mind. With happiness, things in life have to be in balance. Happiness requires elements, whereas peace of mind requires nothing but acceptance. Whether the situation is good or bad, it makes no difference as the mind has already come to terms with what is."

ACHIEVABLE WAYS OF LIVING

Acceptance is peace of mind. You are not happy or frustrated but rather present and aware.
Happiness is something that can be taken away in an instant through a sudden death or a traumatic experience and within seconds...boom! Just like that our happiness no longer exists.

Peace of mind is accepting all factors of life before they have even occurred, be those factors negative or positive. It's the choice to remain composed and centred despite what life throws at you. The mind becomes detached from ego but remains deeply connected, enough to value pain and feel growth.

One of the most important things I've
learned from life is...

_____

_____

_____

_____

_____

_____

_____

_____

_____

_____

_____

_____

ACHIEVABLE WAYS OF LIVING

CHAPTER 6:

IT'S YOU AGAINST YOU...

"Allow yourself to walk bravely into the unknown. Put yourself in a position where you do not know what is next. Learn to tap into new areas of your potential. This will help you discover even more of yourself. In the dark is where there is opportunity to find light."

ACHIEVABLE WAYS OF LIVING

There is something mystical and fascinating about walking into the unknown. The pressure that it comes with is frightening but it shouldn't be enough to hold us back. Exploring a place which has the potential to open up our perspective to a new way of looking at life and ourselves, is an opportunity not to be missed. Take a calculated leap into the unknown. You may just be surprised at what prevails.

"Share what you have with the world. Someone somewhere needs what you have to offer. Your struggle, your pain is somebody's remedy. Heal and teach yourself through healing and teaching others."

ACHIEVABLE WAYS OF LIVING

What you know is liberating to somebody who knows little about what you know. It could be the simplest of things...a piece of information, an insight, a recommendation — all what you think isn't a big deal, but to them, it's a start.

You don't know their hunger or how deep their ambition travels. That could be the piece they've been missing. Knowledge is useless, unless shared or applied. Teach, share and pass on what you know.

"How exciting is it to know you are far from seeing the best version of yourself yet."

ACHIEVABLE WAYS OF LIVING

If this doesn't raise a smile, it needs to. You may find yourself complaining, overwhelmed or even clouded by what's currently going on. Take a step back for a moment and evaluate what's currently going on rather than allowing the mind to take control and perceive the situation as more intense than it is.

It was Seneca who said:
"We suffer more in imagination than we do in reality."

There are going to be times in your life when things are going to be dim, dark and glum. Times as such will have you failing to realise there are greater and more fulfilling days ahead of you. You are doing the best you can with what you've got and it is only going to improve as time goes on. You are not yet a finished product, not as long as my work and I are alive.

"Become a student of life. Learn the lessons of the game. Study the way you think, act and speak. Don't just settle for who you are even if you do not decide to change. At least you know why you are the way you are."

ACHIEVABLE WAYS OF LIVING

Many great lessons are hidden within ourselves. There is a reason you are the way you are. You are not yet a finished product. Underneath your current self is a whole new being. There are many aspects to who you are. Open yourself up and explore you. You'll be amazed at what you discover.

"The laws of life are so simply complicated. There are universal laws, that when you follow them you produce a particular result. That's the simple part. The complicated part is actually following those universal laws."

ACHIEVABLE WAYS OF LIVING

This is the classic case of, 'we know what we should be doing, so why are we not doing it?' - If we know that only after six weeks do we start to see a development within our bodies, why do we remain so inconsistent and not stick around long enough to see our results?

It is really simple but it's complicated. Patience plays a huge part and so does awareness. Being patient enough to see the result and being aware of the process and how it works. Both combined will not only see you stick to it, but generate the result that comes with commitment.

"I want you to know that you have what it takes. You f**king do. I know these words may not emphasise how deeply I'm convinced by this, but please allow yourself to experience this and see for yourself that you do."

ACHIEVABLE WAYS OF LIVING

It's beyond our personal beliefs. It's human nature, a part of our DNA, it's our biological make-up. Of course we have what it takes, the mind is primed and designed for survival. When we have to, believe me we will. It's the effort required that can seem overwhelming and beyond what we think is doable.

Read about stories of what most would consider impossible accomplishments. Human beings are a phenomenal creation. There is a lot still unexplored about the capabilities of the human mind but so far, from what has been achieved through the efforts of individuals has proven that there is a lot left to still figure out about what we can and can't do. Put yourself through the testing and see for yourself that you are more than able to achieve or overcome what you believe to be out of your reach.

"Keep pursuing your goals, even if you are a little confused or struggling to find an answer... maybe you are just not ready yet. Force nothing and persevere through the uncertainty. That push to keep going is the only way you are ever going to get the answer you are looking for."

ACHIEVABLE WAYS OF LIVING

It's never really as straight forward as it seems. It is simple but it is not straight forward. When I first decided to pursue entrepreneurship, 'confused' doesn't even justify how I was feeling.

Then I hit the pad with the pen and centered myself. After intense internal evaluation, this quote was born and everything began to make sense. When you are confused, it is the first step to figuring out the answer. And when you find the answer, you realise it is just the beginning.

"Support yourself. Learn from you, teach you, clap for you. Once you have you, you have everything. Once you learn how to be your own number one fan, external factors have less of an influence upon you. The need to seek approval from others fade. The support and encouragement from others serve a purpose but they don't become the main source, you do!"

ACHIEVABLE WAYS OF LIVING

I write quotes like these when I'm heavily doubting myself. I feel as though people still don't fully appreciate the person I've become and the truth is, they may never. With that being said, I don't think it is their job to appreciate me, it's my job and it's your job to appreciate you.

I suppose that's where our expectations come to bite us. Although I do feel recognition plays a vital role in developing self-worth there is more to it. That 'more' is you. Welcome your own support and embrace your own words of encouragement. Place value upon yourself. Your voice matters.

"This attitude is not common,
it's a mindset which requires deep
introspection, it's looking at things
internally before externally. It's
stepping away from what you see
into what you feel. It's living with the
belief that impossible is
nothing but a personal opinion."

ACHIEVABLE WAYS OF LIVING

This is not a matter of confining to what others expect or believe of you. It's about you taking ownership of your life and choosing to live with the belief that your goals are achievable. This mentality is built of the win/learn concept. In this world there is no such thing as can't or fail. Failure literally doesn't exist!

I say it's not common as people are so easily defeated by setbacks and failure. This mentality is rare but it's adoptable. When you approach life with a win/learn attitude, the possibilities become endless. There is no mountain too high to climb or road too long to travel.

"You can work all your life pursuing wealth in search of happiness and still fall short. You can befriend large amounts of people in search for that one person to provide you love and yet, still feel alone. Or you can look within yourself and be grateful for all areas as they are on this present day. Nothing on the outside can bring happiness unless it is felt from the inside first."

ACHIEVABLE WAYS OF LIVING

'It all falls down to you' is a reoccurring theme throughout this book. I want to emphasise the importance of connecting with yourself as so much stems from there. Once you have found what you are looking for within, your wants and needs lessen and your gratitude grows. Perfect the art of self mastery and your world will transform.

"One of the hardest things about being true to your morals is when a person disrespects you, betrays you or does something where you have to question their integrity. It is still choosing to keep your character in check, despite all the hurt and disappointment you feel. You have to experience the full impact and effect of the pain. Knowing that staying true to you is what matters the most, even though you have every right to act totally out of character."

ACHIEVABLE WAYS OF LIVING

Patience is a gift. The humbleness required when faced with betrayal is admirable. Move on with success, win through healing, as responding negatively only adds more tension to the situation. Channel the energy into something more constructive and beneficial for your mental health.

People will test you and life will challenge you at times when you could do without it. It's unfortunate but it is what it is. Keep your values in check and live with integrity. See it as people leaving your life with bad intentions to make room for clean hearted people to come through with pure intentions. Look at it this way... would you rather be the one healing or the one causing pain?

The accomplishment I'll never forget in my life is...
*(Describe in detail and what
made it so unforgettable?)*

_____

_____

_____

_____

_____

_____

_____

_____

_____

_____

_____

_____

_____

_____

ACHIEVABLE WAYS OF LIVING

Integrity is something I value highly. I mention this word often and more so, I live by it. I feel the purest way to live is by being raw and honest, even if the honesty hurts, it cuts the b******t. Currently, the world is experiencing what most of us have never witnessed before, it's a time of huge confusion and chaos.

People are losing their lives, countries are in lockdown, jobs and businesses are at stake. The whole world is at a standstill. As you've gathered, expressing myself through writing is my thera-py, it's how I heal and channel my energy. After seven months of amazing work, I was told I wouldn't be returning to my place of work due to the closure of the education system. Now if I hadn't been equipped with the composure, resilience or support net-work to keep me feeling optimistic and focused, this is a situa-tion which could have easily caused me to implode. In a way, I'm thankful I've experienced such an event as it has thrown me in at the deep end and forced me to take action on things I may not have moved forward with anytime soon.

I've found it challenging and it is scary to know I'm no longer in a position which provides me with opportunity and financial sta-bilty whilst living in London. I moved to London in August 2019. I came with no connections, only a dream and the energy to make it happen. I'm no stranger to the hardship, I was raised to handle whatever life puts in front of me.

I adore the beauty of adversity. It leaves you no option but to rise to the occasion or deal with the consquences of not adapting to your situation. I've been left with the fear I need to drive me for-ward and ensure there is no room for complacency. I'm deter-minded to continue developing my craft and in my mind, that's final. Although I do have the option of going to seek employment and financial security, I'm just not with it any more, not unless it's a must and a matter of survival. I'm in the deep end now so I may as well carry on swimming, right? I want to focus solely on my mission and this lies in having the opportunity to help shape and be a positive role model for people, to be there for the many young people who lack a significant figure in their lives

I write this with disappointment, but with a heart still full of love and respect. I write to show myself my worth, it has been a humbling experience. Although I thought I knew my worth, it's clear to see there is a lot more for me to learn.
The process been an amazing learning curve and I'm going to take from this what is needed into my next chapter. I had to get this off my chest because I had dark thoughts. My emotions were running wild. It hit hard. With so much uncertainty in the world right now only to realise my world is to become a lot more uncertain.

A new chapter begins. Where do I go from here? To the same destination; just a different route! I can only give thanks for having the opportunity. It was my first interview and my first taste of hustle in London and I'm confident more opportunities will arise. I think it is powerful to share your setbacks, on my behalf, it's considered an L but the bigger picture is, it's probably the most valuable L I've ever taken.

For the first time since 2014, I shed a tear, I sat and I cried for a moment, funny enough with a smile on my face, it has been one hell of a journey so far. Now it's about taking Achievable Ways Of Living forward and pushing to influence and improve more lives. A final note on this topic...I'm giving you my reality as it is. I feel there are important lessons to learn from my experiences, especially in a time like now. As I've told you, being true to who you are is key. On my way home from hearing I won't be returning to work, I sat on the tube lost in thought, my mind going in every direction possible, questioning everything despite all the panic, heartache and the thousand other things I had going on, I decided to hold myself accountable. I had a concept copy of this book saved on my phone. I began flicking through the quotes, putting my work to the test. If there was ever a time to stress test my product, it was now. I sat there reading them with a tear in my eye. I was moved. At a time I needed me, I was there.

I promise you all, if I had sat there and read this book and thought..."Nope! This doesn't bang!" I would have deleted it there and then and called the whole project off. Hand on heart I was touched. This book has more meaning to me now than it ever did — now that this has happened. The meaning attached to it is deeper than starting my journey as an author; it is my pain and passion.

Pages - 11, 27, 85,99, 140, 160

The whole read was hard-hitting but these quotes in particular penetrated my soul. I prayed for this book to land in the hands of the people who need it the most. How ironic is it that the first person hands it landed in were my own.

ACHIEVABLE WAYS OF LIVING

There you have it. Dreams do come true. This is the proof right here. This...what you're holding is a dream. This is more than a book. It's a vision I've had which, through my actions I've manifested into a physical asset. When my pen first touched the page on Thursday 19th March 2015 at John Lennon Airport on my way to visit Barcelona, never did I think, five years later, I'd have a book of my own. This is so far from the path I was travelling. It's magnificent how your life can be shaped with just a little ambition.

As I've reflected upon my writing over the years, it has brought me back to the experiences I was going through around the time each quote was created. When I see how much my attitude and articulation has progressed, it really is inspiring. I have grown tremendously. Due to my tunnel vision and relentlessness, I've failed to realise how much growth has actually occurred.

It happens so fast, when you are going from day to day it's hard to grasp what is actually occuring in the moment. For writing to be my passion...thinking about it deeply...I find it mind blowing. Who would have guessed? I was kicked out of two schools, as well as college. So to now have a book and a brand that represents personal growth and self-empowerment is f**cking crazy. You can't predict the unknown, but I've learnt you can create it. The success of this book is partly beyond my control. For the part that is within my control, I'm going to give it everything.

Now that we have reached the end, I again thank you with all my heart for both making an investment in me and also in yourself. In this book, I've given you as good as I've got at this current stage. No doubt as I continue to create and write, my vocabulary and writing style will improve...more of that in the next up and coming book.

Printed in Great Britain
by Amazon